fourteen songs

by Rabindranath Tagore

learned, translated and introduced at the Bard's wish

by Arthur Geddes

We hope in due course to produce
a CD of the 14 songs in this book.
If you would be interested in
receiving a copy, please inform
marion.geddes@wanadoo.fr.

Published by Resurgence Trust
Ford House, Bideford, Devon EX39 6EE, UK
www.resurgence.org

ISBN 978 0 85784 022 6

Design by Rick Lawrence
rick@samskara-design.com

Printed by Kingfisher Print & Design, Totnes, Devon, UK.

SELECTED PUBLICATIONS BY ARTHUR GEDDES

Au Pays de Tagore, la civilisation rurale du Bengale Occidental. Armand Colin, Paris 1927.

The Songs of Craig and Ben: Lays, laments, love songs and lilts of the mountaineers and cragsmen of the Highlands and Isles, Vols. 1 and 2. William Maclellan, Glasgow 1951 and 1961.

Presenting Tagore in sound and sight. Brochure published for the Tagore centenary exhibition, Adam House, University of Edinburgh, 1961.

Man and Land in South Asia, ed. by A.T.Learmonth, A.M. Learmonth, C.D.Deshpande and L.S.Bhat. Concept Publishing Company, New Delhi 1982.

CORRESPONDENCE BETWEEN ARTHUR GEDDES AND RABINDRANATH TAGORE
A Meeting of Two Minds: Geddes Tagore letters, edited and introduced by Bashabi Fraser. Revised edition, Word Power Books, 2005. (Although most of the correspondence is between Rabindranath Tagore and Patrick Geddes, it includes some between Tagore and Arthur Geddes.)

CONTENTS

DARTINGTON HALL.
TOTNES, DEVON.

7th July, 1930.

I have great pleasure in testifying
to the accuracy of my melodies and songs
which Mr. Arthur Geddes has taken down in
staff notation, and I hope, for my own sake,
that he will continue this work and help me
in giving permanence to my musical composition
by taking down in a system of notation which
is universally accepted.

INTRODUCTION

Marion Geddes and Claire Geddes

Our father, Arthur Geddes (1895–1968), died before completing this book. He would probably have made some minor alterations to his text, particularly to the notes accompanying the individual songs. He also planned to include a final section on the modes and rhythms of the melodies, similar to the text accompanying his translations of Gaelic songs from Scotland, published in 'The Songs of Craig and Ben', Vol.2, pp.74–81 (William Maclellan, Edinburgh 1961). However, we believe that the text presented here is very close to the final form he would have wished to hand over to his publisher. An agreement to publish the book was made with Max Hinrichsen of London, in 1962. However, steady rises in costs and changes in the market soon made publication impossible.

From 1921 to 1924 Arthur Geddes was in India assisting the town-planning work of his father Patrick Geddes, and the rural reconstruction projects of Rabindranath Tagore at Sriniketan. It was during this period that he learned Bengali, sang and made notations of some of Tagore's songs and played the melodies on his violin. He later graduated in geography and published his doctoral thesis 'Au Pays de Tagore' at the University of Montpellier, France, where from 1925 to 1927 he was also contributing to his father's work at the College des Ecossais. He then returned to his native Scotland and worked in the Department of Geography at Edinburgh University until 1965. During this time he published many research papers on the human geography of India. Some of these papers were incorporated in a book, unfinished at the time of his death but subsequently edited by Professor A.T.M. Learmonth et al and published as 'Man and Land in South Asia' (Concept Publishing Company, New Delhi 1982).

He greatly admired Rabindranath Tagore and continued to share and raise awareness of Tagore's poems and songs at home and abroad. We hope that our father's rendering of Tagore's songs in this publication will bring pleasure to new audiences.

FOREWORD

by Jawaharal Nehru, Prime Minister of India (1947–1964) and Chancellor of Visva-Bharati, Santiniketan

I am glad to learn that Dr Arthur Geddes is publishing some of the favourite songs of Rabindranath Tagore in English with their own melodies. Geddes, many years ago, published some of Tagore's melodies, which met with the poet's approval. I feel sure that the new publication of 'Fourteen Songs' will be equally welcomed in India and abroad.

Tagore was a remarkable and full-sided personality and the appreciation of his writings and of him as a man has continued to grow all over the world. In India he is know as Gurudev, the great teacher, and his best memorial is the University he founded in Santiniketan. One of his songs has become the National Anthem of India ever since independence. In Bengal he is particularly known and loved because of his songs which have gone down to the villages. The partition of India and Bengal has not affected in any way the great appreciation of his writings, and especially his songs, in both parts of Bengal. To us in India, he is looked upon as one of the Rishis or Seers of old who carried on the ancient tradition in modern times. His influence over successsive generations has been very great, even though it has not had the glamour and publicity attached to the successful politician; yet his influence was much deeper and will continue when the politician's name is hardly remembered.

Tagore and Gandhi overlapped for many years and were the outstanding representatives of India. They were different in many ways and sometimes criticised each other's views and activities, but yet they were drawn to each other, and each of them had great regard and affection for the other. It was fascinating to see these two men of great stature, representing different aspects of India, and both of them even though appreciating and understanding many modern trends yet representing fundamentally the old spirit of India.

Tagore was essentially a singer and it is perhaps easier to understand him through his songs than through his writings. I welcome, therefore, this publication by Dr Geddes and hope this will make the spirit of Tagore better known in West and East.

COMMENTS ON THE TRANSLATIONS

Muhammad Abdul Hai, Head of the Department of Bengali, University of Dhaka, East Pakistan (1962)

As Arthur Geddes rightly felt when forty years ago he learned, enjoyed, played and sang the songs of Tagore, his friend and teacher, Rabindranath was a 'singer, melodist and poet in one'; in a single Celtic word a Bard, the best-loved Bard of the two Bengals, East and West. The songs of Tagore – many of the melodies of which were never written down direct from his singing – are handed down among us by living tradition. Here are fourteen songs of which the Bard enjoyed the hearing and formally approved the transcription, and which he asked Arthur Geddes to translate into simple English.

The songs in this book tell of courage and calm, of truth and tenderness, of solitude and human love, and the search for the Divine. And of death there is an awareness, but not fear. The images that spring to the mind's eye of a Bengali as he sings or listens to these songs are those of our people, and our near and dear ones. Yet as Tagore the Bard knew, these are but forms of the universal.

As a Bengali, knowing each of the songs in words and melody, I realise that the mode and the rhythm of the melodies assist in resetting the words in an utterly different language, different in its syllables and spoken rhythms. I found myself approaching the translations with some apprehension, even though I know they were made at the Bard's wish and begun with his encouragement and approval. As Arthur Geddes conceives it, a translator's problem is threefold. It is first to suggest the conception, deep in the Poet's being – his subconscious; next to convey the scenes of the Poet's experience – the plants and creatures, waters and skies, from dawn to dark; and last, to carry over the rhythms and hint at the word-sounds of the original. Let me take these three problems in their turn, as they have been faced in these songs.

Since Rabindranath was first and last a human being, the conceptions which well up in his songs lie deep in the human heart. The words in which he expressed them are of course in our own speech. Yet in song his words transcend any single tradition and are not bound down to Hindu thoughts alone but on the contrary are linked to Muslim and Christian mystical experiences, and to the devotional songs of Kabir, the Punjabi weaver. The Poet was surely a master of humanist thought and also of English prose, and hence these songs do offer the possibility of re-expression in a European language. Geddes was helped by his friendship and to a great extent he has succeeded. But where he felt his verse failed, he has made this clear in the story or note to a song, where a more literal translation will be found.

Secondly, the things that we see around us and the images of our land have associations for us which are absent say to a Marathi, still more to a European. Yet, just as we felt on first reading poetry in English the delight of imagining sights we had never seen, so a European may find in these songs the pleasure of discovery.

Tagore was a keen observer and liked to name a particular tree, plant or flower in song. And here a translator can help the imagination by a descriptive word or phrase. In the last song 'Santiniketan', it is enough for a Bengali that the Bard should simply name its trees, for at once we can see them. But knowing and loving Santiniketan, Geddes realised that a stranger must be made aware of the tallness of the sal, of the forests or the feathery foliage and quiet coloured flowering of the amlaki. We know the sound of the sitar to which we sing and so, almost unconsciously, we sense the Poet's allusion to voices attuned to it in unison, and hear its 'love strings', which though untouched, ring when a player plucks the strings above them. In two or three words the translation hints at this and in the 'story' makes clear the lovely image of the Poet's ideal, which he sought to realise in the life of Santiniketan.

Tagore's verses are rich in allusions and metaphors, and the English critic Edward Thompson complained of their number, forgetting perhaps that in surroundings familiar to us the allusions can be instantly understood and that many metaphors may be part of our daily speech.

Since singing calls for clear sounds and instant comprehension the translator may have to choose and lay stress on essential images. So in this book, when details are omitted, they will be found in the notes, as in those to the first song 'O the gateways of the South…let fling'. Thus the full imagery is restored for every poem.

Lastly, the English can be enjoyed as verse I feel. In Bengali most syllables end in vowel sounds, as will be clear even from the Bengali song titles. But in English most words end in consonants. Our flowing rhymes and open singing vowels are features which a Bengali listener misses, but the loss is inevitable when English is to be sung.

And here Tagore's own wish was clear and strong. He wished one whose own language was English to make some new song versions to be sung. It was only after forty years that Geddes made his first attempt to carry out Tagore's request. It was only after practice over thirty years in translating Gaelic songs of his own land, such as Tagore loved to hear, that he felt able to fulfil his old friend's wish.

In his foreword Mr Nehru has expressed his hope that this book will make the spirit of Tagore better known in 'India and abroad', and indeed English is a world language.

```
                                        Comilla
                                  18 February 1926

Dear Arthur

How delighted to have your letter.  Do whatever you like with my songs; only
do not ask me the impossible. To translate Bengali poems into English verse
form reproducing the original rhythm so that the words may fit in with the
theme would be foolish for one to attempt.  All that I can venture to do is
render them in simple prose making it possible for a worthier person than my-
self to versify them.  Please write the accompaniment yourself.  I can trust
you, for you are modest and are not likely to smother my tunes with a ruthless
display of your own musical talent.  I shall be able to give the outline of
the play from which the songs are taken in order to give them their proper back-
ground.  As for other details, I shall have them discussed when we meet in Eu-
rope.

Just now I am busy touring in East Bengal.  It is perfectly unwise from med-
ical point of view but there are other points of view in its favour which it
has been difficult for me to ignore.

But I am tired and am longing to give up missions of all kinds and merely to
share the life and impulse of the trees and birds in this delightful spring-
time redolent of mango blossoms.

With love,

Yours affectionately,

Rabindranath Tagore
```

Letter published in 'A Meeting of Two Minds: Geddes Tagore Letters', edited and introduced by Bashabi Fraser. p.121 revised edition. Word Power Books, 2005.

RABINDRANATH TAGORE

HIS LIFE AND WORK

Rabindranath Tagore was born in Calcutta on May 7 1861, and died there on August 7 1941.

This span of eighty years covered a life of incessant and many-sided creative activity which made him one of the outstanding figures of his age. In India itself he stood as an eminence equalled only by Gandhi. And in the rest of the world he was acclaimed as a noble and authentic voice of the East.

Perhaps the strongest influence on him in his formative years was that of his own family. His father and grandfather were both leaders of the nineteenth century Renaissance in India; their home was a centre of the intellectual life of the period. Brought up in this environment, Rabindranath was steeped from childhood in the best traditions of an ancient culture that was quickening under the touch of western science, technology, governance and enterprise. Rabindranath died before his country became free. Moreover the Second World War was raging at the time, and this, added to the memories of the First, clouded his last days with increased misgivings about western civilisation. But we must not forget that his was, above all, the 'Religion of Man'. He never lost faith in man's capacity to rise from the ashes of tragedy and build his life anew.

Rabindranath started writing before he was fifteen, and by the time he reached his early twenties he had already established himself as a prolific author gifted with a rare power of expression and rich and fruitful imagination. From then on, until the very end, he continued to write and publish, mostly in Bengali, his mother tongue, an enormous amount of work which before long left no one in doubt that here was a Master, or Gurudev as they say in India – not only a master of language, but of music and the truth and beauty that words can convey.

At the age of twenty-nine his father sent 'Rabi' to take charge of family estates in north-east Bengal. There he came to know the villagers, their sufferings and their problems of cultivation, of credit and marketing. Shocked by the poverty he found, a first impulse had

been to refuse to collect the rents and taxes due to his family and government. But the outstanding progress on the estates he administered is on record, as in the official District Gazetteer of Rajshahi (1911). Tagore saw that too often the cultivators came to him or to the District Collector (head government official) to plead, not to work as freemen together. Let us review three aspects of his life : his songs , dramas and prose, his educational initiatives, and his practical leadership.

The sheer volume of his output is impressive. Essays, plays, poems, short stories, novels, and disquisitions on social and philosophical themes – in all an estimated total of some seventeen thousand closely printed pages, only a part of which is available in English. Of poems alone there are over one thousand, and two thousand songs besides, written and set to music by Tagore himself. Indeed, he was a musician of the highest order who began as a traditionalist but soon expanded his range to include elements from western music and fuse them with his eastern background. He took to painting when he was nearing seventy and yet produced within ten years almost three thousand pictures, some of which critics have judged to be among the finest paintings of his time in India.

Rabindranath first visited England in 1877, when he was sixteen, and throughout his life he cherished a deep admiration for the British people and many aspects of British life. It was in England too, in 1912, that the world discovered him. His book of poems 'Gitanjali', published in England, was instantly hailed as a work of profound beauty and wisdom, and formal international recognition quickly came with the award of the Nobel Prize for Literature in 1913.

In the following years, and particularly in the decade between 1920 and 1930, Rabindranath travelled extensively and often, in the Far East, in Europe and America. The whole world had now become his audience, and everywhere he went he was received with enthusiasm and made countless friends by his presence, speech and song. He visited the Soviet Union in 1930 and was favourably impressed by much that he saw.

'More than any other Indian', as Pandit Jawarahal Nehru has written, 'he helped to bring into harmony the ideas of the East and West. He was India's international-ist par excellence, believing in and working for international cooperation, taking India's message to other countries and bringing their message to his own people. Tagore, the aristocratic artist turned democrat with pro-letarian sympathies, represented essentially the cultural tradition of India, the tradition of accepting life in the fullness thereof and going through it with song and dance.'

And, as Nehru said, 'Although politically I followed Gandhi, in ideas I owe still more to Tagore'.

Rabindranath believed passionately in Indian inde-pendence, but instead of plunging into the turmoil of po-litical conflicts, he concentrated on strengthening what he conceived to be the basis of effective national freedom – a fearless and self-reliant people, To this end, he de-voted much time and thought to education and the prob-lems of social reform. He founded the famous school at Santiniketan where, some years later, he established the university Visva-Bharati, i.e. 'Universal-and-Indian' or 'International-National'.

In one sense Tagore's message was that of an arch-rebel. His preoccupation with the concept of Freedom, his contempt for slavish conformity exacted by and of-fered to external forces, and the dead traditions of a by-gone age, this was in part aesthetic and moral in its inspiration . It was the poet's proud assertion of his in-dividuality. But running through much of his writings is also the conviction that if a new social order is to be built, in India or elsewhere, it can only be by a coura-geous rejection of outworn laws and institutions, and an intelligent application of science to human values.

As a youth Tagore had eagerly read of science and among his finest disciples were young scientists. Early in the century Tagore had purchased a farm and out-buildings for experiment and demonstration near Santi-niketan. In turn he sent his son, adopted son and son-in-law to agricultural colleges in America, to train them to take charge, and this they began. Then Tagore brought a young British ex-serviceman, Leonard Elmhirst, who in 1922 settled on the farm with a keen team of Bengali workers. They started to train students, and then by example to teach the Hindu and Moslem vil-lagers and schoolmasters, and their children, new ways of living together. Prime tasks were to restore fertility and grow better crops, improve essential crafts and achieve cooperation. This was Sriniketan, 'Home of Prosperity'. They met with difficulties, overcome by hard work – and by laughter! National efforts for rural re-newal in the 1960s in India, Pakistan and Ceylon owe more to Tagore than to any other single man.

THE SINGER AND HIS SONGS

This first fulfilment of Rabindranath's wish, a book of his songs to sing in a language which is ours and the world's, makes this little work unique. I rejoice, yet grieve, to find it so. For I am glad that this is done which is asked, from when first he knew me until the last time we met. Yet I grieve that we failed to bring it off in his lifetime, so that he died believing it might never be done. 'Nothing', he said to me early one morning in 1923, 'nothing gives me the same sense of attainment, of achievement, as the making of a song!' His joy in the making and singing of a song, and the joy of fellow-singers who sang with him in his song dramas, this was wonderful to share. Al-though now tragically severed by politicians' frontiers, people in all Bengal gather to sing his songs, at home and together in the open, in village and town. Where else in the world may you traverse a great city at sunset and see old and young gather spontaneously at every second or third street to sing, on his anniversary, the songs of their own national bard?

Yet, as an intimate mutual Bengali friend told me when we went over these fourteen songs together, Ra-bindranath would say in his last years to her and other friends, 'That my songs will vanish is the tragedy of my life. For in Bengal, in India, they may be distorted, either by variations in classical style or commonplace mis-shaping. They will not be my songs.' And to me he grieved that his songs should remain unknown in the wider world. Although his flowing and suggestive ren-derings into English prose were acclaimed and were re-translated into many languages at second or third hand, so far as we can learn they were never translated anew, directly from his expressive Bengali, to their own melodies. At least fifteen European composers have published their own settings to his English prose-renderings or to retranslations of these, and I know others unpublished, But never until now were his songs translated to be sung to the melodies which were those of his people, of his own inspiration and his singing.

Here then are but fourteen of some two thousand songs which flowed from him in the modal melody and singing speech of his native land, Bengal. The words are translated direct, often with his help, to as close a fusion of their inward concepts, vivid imagery, rhythms and verse forms as I could combine. Surely this may be but a beginning, and other and better translators of his songs may now come forward or be found

To renew a great friendship is a profound pleasure, as now it is to fulfil the friend's behest, first made in 1923. It was when I came to share in rural reconstruction at Sriniketan and teach at the nascent university of Santiniketan that Tagore, still young at sixty-two, became known to me, as an initiator, a master blest – Gurudev, an inspiring collaborator, and lifelong a dedicated learner of whatever friends spontaneously offered, were they child, woman or man. He had invited me to teach and apply the enlivening study of 'Folk at Work in their Place',[1] leading to the inter-relationship of a 'Community cooperating in achievement'.

The land, the 'Place', was fascinating. From its open, red-soiled upland, Santiniketan looks over the wide rice plain of Bengal, with its groves and villages of Hindus and Muslims. Westward the upland merges into the hills and vales of India's north eastern plateau, with its friendly animistic tribesfolk, the Santals, so that groups of all three communities dwell near one another. The encouragement of my studies there led to my first work on that land, 'Au Pays de Tagore'. But Tagore's first collaboration with me came when, in the spirit of Sri- and Santiniketan, I sought to dramatise the making, ruin and remaking of the land in 'A Masque of Earth and Man'. Delighted and unasked, the Bard not only retaught the young folk some of his songs they knew, but composed and taught new songs. After it was played, by 'students' and Santals, he urged me to write out the Masque for the first volume of his Visva-Bharati Quarterly. Such was Gurudev, singer, teacher and inspiring friend.

Meanwhile I witnessed him producing one of his song dramas on Spring, and went to Calcutta with more

than a score of children and young folk who were rehearsing, chattering or sleeping on the arcaded verandahs of the stately family home. That young folk, not only men but girls and women, should actually play, sing and dance together, in public, was an act of social revolution which they accomplished by the sheer joy they took in it, so converting their shocked elders to new vision!

It was in the Khasi Hills that my host first sang some of his finest songs to me. Hearing them on the violin, whose expressive tone is loved in India, finding that I was writing down the melodies and learning words by heart, and also liking my occasional verse, he suggested that I translate them to be sung in English. Shakily I tried my hand and naturally I failed, although by his help my drafts were to prove useful later. A few of the melodies I wrote down were published by a mutual friend, Andrée Karpelès, in her fine selection 'L'Inde et son âme' (1928).

In 1930, when the guest of Leonard Elmhirst in Dartington, Devon, Tagore wired me to come and continue collaboration. After we had parted he formally recorded his wishes as to melody (see page 4). He also read and approved the introductions I had written to his songs and encouraged me in my search for a worthy translator and a publisher, a search unhappily made in vain. Again in 1938 at Santiniketan, when he was nearly eighty, yet still a vigorous producer, we tried to carry out his wish, still unsuccessfully. He died in 1941.

It may be asked 'Why then did the Poet not publish the melodies he wrote?' The answer is simple: it was because he could not write them, musically he was illiterate. The inward strength of Rabindranath was not merely that of a reader but of a listener, and not that of a 'writer' of music but of an oral singer through who there flowed the stream of his country's melodies, season by season, from dawn through noon to starlight. In the Introduction to the words of over two hundred songs, without their melodies, in the collection 'Prabahini' (Calcutta 1926) Rabindranath wrote: 'The poems which are published in this 'Prabahini' are all songs, full of melody, (*sure bhadani*, 'bound up with music'). For this reason, in some stanzas there may not be proper rhythm (or metre). In spite of this, I believe that this book could be read as an enduring song-sequence (*gite-kabe*)'.

---

1. A reference to 'Folk, Work, Place', the regional survey method used by Arthur Geddes's father, Patrick Geddes (eds).

THE BARD : THREE SOURCES

Rabindranath was not merely a 'poet', but singer-melodist-poet in one, truly a 'bard'. Having attempted translation into verse in a foreign language, English, he felt his endeavours were inadequate. Hence he simply fell back on writing the prose renderings in English from which translations were made into a score of European and Indian languages. Lovely as these are – or they would not have stirred the world as they did from their first publication in 1912 until depression, darkness and then war mania overcame the western world in the 1930s – these too he knew were inadequate. They failed to render the vivid strength of his imagery, the masterly form and word music of his sung verse. And without their melody, they remained mere prose poetry, not songs – lyric, ballad, meditative chant or joyous song with unison chorus. Thus he asked me for three things. First, being musically illiterate and unable to write down his melodies, that they be written down. Second, that they be translated for singing. And hence that they be sung, to their own words in English.

Steeped in the living tradition of his native land and people, learned also in the hereditary, ultra-refined scholarship of classical melody, this singer of Bengal was both freed and enriched from a further source: the expressiveness of singing in the western world. It is the confluence of these three streams which composed the flowing river of his song-making. His songs moved all who heard. Under the open sky, in village hut or pillared civic home, in intimacy or in the pageantry of drama, their hearing was unforgettable.

Yet let it not be supposed that though Indian hearers might be moved, they were undisturbed or untroubled. Far from Tagore's songs being instantly approved by his fellow countrymen, many of his melodies met with disapproval, for example from the pandits because they broke classical rules, and from others also. These were accustomed either to village strains, which caste, urbanisation and 'anglicisation' had too often led them to disdain, or to the conventional, stilted limitation of melodic elaboration by a singe voice – too often painfully stretched to throaty harshness. Of this national fault Tagore has recorded his criticisms.

Singing in parts, in polyphony, was of course still absent. The substitute was recently described by the musical critic of a sensitive Bengali singer as the 'drab monotonous line' of the tambala, the 'twanging, droning string-base on the tonic and dominant', with the syncopated 'tapping-thump' of the teacher's or accompanist's finger-beaten drum, his tabla. Unless a melody is composed for a drone so that its notes are conceived as forming rudimentary discord and chord by turns as in a tune composed for the bagpipes, surely a drone dulls and disfigures it. Although Tagore never attempted music other than melody, with unison chorus when he wished, he enjoyed part-singing as when sung to him by students in Vienna. And in maturity he never sang to a base or drone. Except for experiments in youth, still less would he sing to the monotonous notes of the hand organ or harmonium, played with the right hand and 'pedalled' with the left. Commonly used in India for the last hundred years, this not only obliterates the finer transitional intervals of pure melody – Indian, Gaelic or other – but stifles expression. It is unfortunate that use of the harmonium was tolerated in Santiniketan, for this must be partly responsible for the decay in expressive singing by children and adults which I felt in later visits. And while mere unison of voice and harmonium (with approximate synchronisation) is bad enough, it is still worse when a player slips in an occasional third below the melody, regardless and often destructive of the mode or raga. This one too often hears done to Tagore's songs.

As many of the Bard's lovely melodies, orally transmitted, have been rendered for years in such ways, it is little wonder that not only have they suffered in expressiveness, but that some have lost their rhythm, mode or both and are only heard in bowdlerised forms. Happily, not only are there a few old gramophone records and worn but authentic tapes of the Bard's own singing; there are singers, old and young, who still convey something of the Bard's own spell. And since Rabindranath, when he produced one of his song dramas with himself as an actor, could joyously lead, in fact 'conduct' the young folk, many Bengalis trained by Bengali teachers could rise to sing expressively, if 'led' as Gurudev would lead.

As said, Rabindranath's melody and singing flowed from three sources : from the songs of village, field and river, from classical tradition and from the west. As a youth in London about 1880, Tagore took lessons in singing. As a result his family and friends were shocked on his return and they exclaimed, he wrote : 'Our Rabi sings in a funny foreign way!' Yet before long he had shed whatever was intrinsically false – as so much was in

English Victorian singing. A quiet humility made him ready to learn, self-respect could help him to reject and humour chased away false sentiment!

A nightly comedy was played to me when, just before her bedtime, Tagore's little grand-daughter, still too young to speak, would be set down on the carpet where he sat, to hear him sing. Bright eyed, she waited. With no more than a side glance at me, Grandfather would begin, tempo andantino, con molto sentimento. 'If lo-ove were like the rose is, and you-ou were like the leaves, Our lives would grow together, like ---'. Like what, I never learned. For about this point grand-daughter would knit her little brows, shake her tiny fists to and fro until Grandfather, with almost pained regret (well feigned) and with a look of deepest apology to me that this tiny one could not rise to the heights of Victorian emotion, would cease. He would pause a moment to make a fresh choice, while we waited, wondering but knowing there would be no more English. A favourite was the tale of the Frog, happily crawk-crawking by a pond, a tank, when spying him, the S-s-snake approached with serpentine s-sinuous glide saying gr-r-rimly 'I'll swallow you down'. Then Froggie : 'But I'll go plop, Plop, PLOP! into the tank and down to the very bottom!' – which he did! Next, Grandfather would sing some lovely little song of his own, to her evident delight – and his – and to my supposed discomfiture!

Yes, before long young Rabi had shed the false to seek the true. Yet through life he kept what was best in what he had learned : to relax his throat, which allowed him to sing without strain, covering two tenor octaves where he had so composed, and with never a false start but true to pitch from the first unguided note. He had admirable control of volume, increasing or diminishing as feeling led or willed. And with this he linked the characteristic Indian art of delicate melodic ornament and of transitional passing 'quarter-tones', two features recalling our native Gaelic singing.

1861–1961

In the British Isles in 1961, a hundred years after the Bard's birth, two generations listened with surprise to the songs of Tagore. One was the generation over sixty who knew the prose renderings in their youth but who in the end became dissatisfied with them They felt a lack of form and rhythm, a weakness of imagery, and repetitions, not realising that he was far more dissatisfied with these renderings than ever they could be! The younger generation, in their twenties, had never heard of him but now heard his songs sung with a sense of discovery, And while for the older generation – and still more perhaps for the in-betweens – there is a certain cloud of prejudice to clear before rediscovery can dawn, there is none among the younger. Here is a fresh field. What is true of Britain seems true of Continental Europe and the Americas.

The 1961 centenary celebrations in every land, from the Americas to the Soviet Union, and from Ireland to China, made the name of Tagore known afresh, yet still too faintly. 'Homage' was offered to the name of one who always refused homage, refused on the dual grounds, I feel, of humility and of self- and mutual respect. Not homage, but enjoyment of his joys and sharing of his sorrows, as in his songs he felt and told the sorrows of others – surely this was what he sought in mortal life? This we should seek, to enter into whatever is ever-living, immortal in his life. Let us share in 'attainment'. If we desire it, enjoy it, let us take part in the re-making of his songs, by singing them afresh, in his language if we know it, or as he also wished, in our own but with the splendour, the flow and the colour of his finest melodies. Choice is important. We need what was best from him and also what is and can be best to us, best for ourselves and one another.

Among his own people from end to end of Bengal, his songs are sung. But in the rest of India, Pakistan and Ceylon, his work is known through its veil of English prose, among the 'literary'. The translation of his songs for singing is important for 'India' as he loved it, undivided from 'Sind and the Punjab, to the Dravidian South, and from Indus to Padma and Brahmaputra!' For his are songs whose feelings all true 'Indians' can understand. How far is this true of our own nation and people? To a greater extent, I believe, than has yet been realised by colleagues, Indian or English. Even the prose renderings had their admirers among working men, such as a sawyer's labourer I knew in the High Street of Edinburgh, although the sheer absence of privacy in those days made them harder to enjoy for one ill-housed as he was.

What of the songs? Going to the London 1961 Centenary celebrations, I shared a sleeper with a vigorous young Scots mechanic in the Forces. He had 'never heard of Tagore', but when I passed him my song translations he read 'March Alone!' with growing attention and was pleased, when I lilted the air, by the vigour and snap of the 'bagpipe' mode and rhythm, but still more by its message. Then, one by one, he read the poems, deeply intent. And at the end he said, 'What a deeply religious man! Of all, I like best 'Oh my master, I know not Thy own singing'.'

If further celebrations are to be truly national and international not one poet but a team, perhaps a growing host of singer-poets, is needed, each choosing what to him is most stirring, most significant. There is place for the hearing and publication of western musical compositions whether to Tagore's prose renderings, or to verse such as Edward Thompson's thoughtful and well wrought versions (1924, 1928).. Yet, above all, let the translators include poets who sing to his melodies, themselves true bards, true to Rabindranath's own flowing genius.

During his lifetime Tagore felt strongly that, as in so many forms of human endeavour, thought and art, the songs of India and the west should both free and enrich one another. What was true then is still truer now, although his own inspired fusion, his deliberate synthesis of western and eastern, of British and Bengali traditions is no longer growing as when he sang. It is for those who had the joyous privilege of learning from his singing to enlist those who can and will sing the best of his splendid songs, and in their way make them known internationally. And it may be that in Scotland or Ireland singers with the strength and limitations of an almost purely melodic native tradition will prove naturally suited to fulfil the Bard's own wish and carry his songs out to a wider world.

It seems astonishing that these fourteen translations of Tagore's songs appear to be the first made from the Bengali to their own airs, whether into English or any European international language. No blame falls upon Bengalis for not achieving this. As Professor Buddhadeva Bose – himself a translator of Baudelaire into Bengali – has stressed, translation of poetry comes best into one's own tongue, not from it. Song must be understood, both as words to melody and as melody to words. And the understanding of melody and words comes best when the art is highest.

Tagore felt that song should be a universal art, as it was when he sang. This was true both for the language of melody and its singing. As these songs show, it was the songs of his people in their thatched homes which moved him, rather than those of pandits in palaces of which the gracefully curved pavilions imitate the curves of thatch. Few of his songs follow the intricate scales, the ragas, elaborated by classical musicians. They are composed mainly in variants of the five fundamental modes, readily named from their chief note, usually the first accented note and the final doh – most frequently with re and mi, sol and la. And, unless he was seated beside a child on the floor, I never heard him sing with diaphragm cramped from sitting cross-legged on the ground. At home he would sing seated on a chair but erect. Before an audience he would stand. And he moved freely when he chanted or sang in his song dramas. In 1912 he wrote of the singing of an Englishwoman, Mrs Ananda Coomaraswamy : 'First she sang European folk songs with piano accompaniment. They were delightful... Then Indian songs, sung with all their richness of details, depth of feeling and exquisite modulations... Yet her voice was her own and could not be mistaken for Indian. The casket was as perfect as the gem.'

I. FIVE SONGS FROM THE SONG DRAMA 'RAJA', 'THE KING OF THE DARK CHAMBER'

Here are five songs from one song drama which were learned and noted during the production by Tagore in Santiniketan and Calcutta in 1924. From these, linked by narrative, may be felt the sequence of lyric chains in Tagore's dramas.

The dramas of India were usually sustained with song, and the village jatras (folk entertainment) are in great part chanted. Tagore however used speech for his action throughout, and his lyrics express the emotion to which speech and action have led. Sometimes it is one of the active figures of the play who sings, or a group of players may sing in chorus. And in certain plays, as in 'Sacrifice', a singer appears who has no part in the play but moves across its strands, somewhat like a single figure from a Greek chorus, not in the play yet of it, and lifting the action of the play by her song from the immediate to the eternal. In 'The King of the Dark Chamber' there is one character, a Serving Maid, who, with a minor part in the action of the play, seems even closer to the inmost voice of the Poet, who played the Grandfather, singing joyously with his Boys and Girls, than any of the characters who seem to dominate the action.

'The King of the Dark Chamber' is an allegory whose feeling and philosophy is deeply India's and suffused with the passion of her highest quest, yet never divorced from humanity, love and youth.

The play opens with Wayfarers arriving in a delectable land for the festival, soon to be held in it. 'And where?' they ask. 'Everywhere!' is the answer, as a troop of boys headed by Grandfather come running in and sing 'Oh the gateways of the south are opening… Come, oh my spring!'

OH THE GATEWAYS OF THE SOUTH . . . . LET FLING!
Amir basanta . . . . eso he!

Allegro - joyfully

But as they run off fresh doubts arise, and the Wayfarers ask 'Where is the king of the country and when is he to appear?' and their insistence infects the people, who ask Grandfather, 'Surely he should appear. His absence is just one big gap!' 'Gap?' cries Grandfather, and sings with the boys 'Oh, we're rajas-royal, one and all…'.

OH, WE'RE RAJAS-ROYAL, ONE AND ALL!
Amra sabai Raja

Allegro
Chorus (with great force and joy)

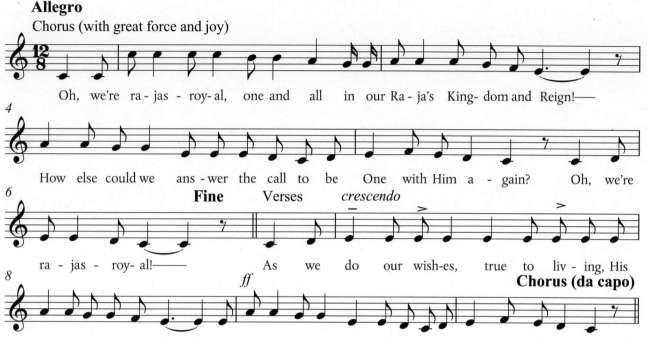

Oh, we're ra - jas - roy-al, one and all in our Ra - ja's King- dom and Reign!——

How else could we ans - wer the call to be One with Him a - gain? Oh, we're

Fine Verses *crescendo*

ra - jas - roy- al!—— As we do our wish-es, true to liv - ing, His

ff **Chorus (da capo)**

life's ful-fill-ing our lives, —— we're nev-er, ne - ver bound by fear to a king who's king of slaves!

Let no untruth betray, enthral,	Though a surging river flood dismay
Nor ever dishonour bring:	With eddies dragging our feet
Our Raja honours each and all	Forward! ford it! do not stray:
And through All, the Inner King!	In the Royal Way we'll meet!
Chorus	*Chorus*

A few of the Wayfarers and of the people have understood. Yet others murmur and a stranger whispers, 'There can be no King. These people have somehow kept the rumour afloat!' Quietly the Serving Maid of the baffled bride-Queen, who cannot find her King, sings 'Deep in my heart He dwells'.

DEEP IN MY HEART
Ontare jagicha ontarjami

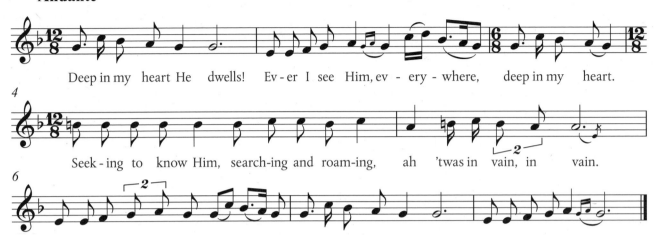

Andante

Deep in my heart He dwells! Ev-er I see Him, ev-ery-where, deep in my heart.

Seek-ing to know Him, search-ing and roam-ing, ah 'twas in vain, in vain.

Deep in my eyes, my grief, be-hold Him; deep in my heart He dwells, ev-er and ev-er-more.

By now we understand that the mysterious 'Dark Chamber' is the human soul, and the baffled Queen is in each one of us who seeks God, too often misled by an illusion. And Tagore himself, outwardly the joyous Grandfather with his happy children, more intimately seeks to serve the soul in each of us.

Suddenly there are cries of 'Stand off! Room there! The King is coming!' and, with the triumphal entry of a splendid figure in scarlet and gold, the crowd, entranced, bow before the procession they help to swell. Surely this is the King and at last the Grandfather too will bow? But Grandfather still laughs and will not believe, and in a frolic his truant band go off, laughing yet questing still.

The second scene opens in the Dark Chamber of the palace where the bride-Queen, in tears for the lack of light, makes her complaint to her confidante the Serving Maid. But the Maid answers, 'How can I bring light to a place He would always have kept dark?' And she sighs 'Night fills my window, no lamp shall I light there'.

NIGHT FILLS MY WINDOW
Ratri eshe jethae meshe diner parabaare

Andante espressivo

Night fills my win - dow, —— no lamp shall I light there.

List' - ning from depths of the dark - ness, shall I hear Thy words to bloom in long - ing,

flower through night? ———— Heart of mine fly a - way ——

Soar where Thy stars play sounds of light. Night fills my win - dow.

Days pass in seeking, in search of the way's end.
Ah, though the distant horizon's blurred and
Though I know not hopes I long for,
Still I stay.
Night fills my window, no lamp shall I light there.

And now the Queen sighs for one sight of her liege lord and in tears ask what he looks like. When the King comes he cries 'Open the door, I await.' And the Maid answers 'Will ye not burst open the door and enter your own home, unbidden?' He opens the door for the Queen, who is left standing, alone, still in darkness, before the King. The King remains invisible throughout the play. Again the Queen implores him to let himself be seen by her, and at last, conceding, he says 'Tomorrow evening at the festival you shall see me, but you must recognise me. I shall show myself again and again'. 'I shall know you!' cries the Queen, rejoicing that her heart's wish is to come true. But the Maid, returning, sings 'Whither wayward flying'.

WHITHER WAYWARD FLYING?
Kotha baire doore jaye re oore hae re hae

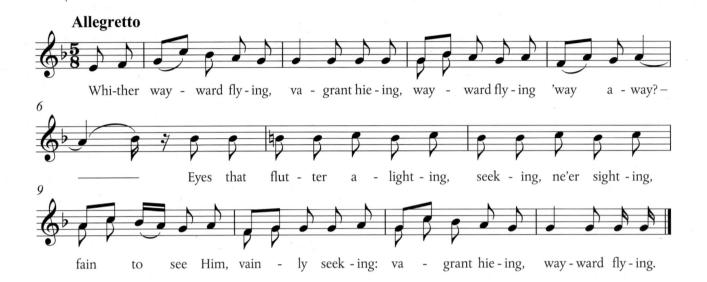

Allegretto

Whi-ther way - ward fly - ing, va - grant hie - ing, way - ward fly - ing 'way a - way? –

————— Eyes that flut - ter a - light - ing, seek - ing, ne'er sight - ing,

fain to see Him, vain - ly seek - ing: va - grant hie - ing, way - ward fly - ing.

Ah, thy heart, that list'ning, hears one singing,
Sounds of singing, 'way, away.
To the wilderness, creeping, wondering, weeping,
Failing, ne'er finding, anguish near blinding,
Faint from trying, Death's voice crying!

Yet, unseen, a Comer, soon, ere summer,
Heard on the south wind, soon, ere May;
Hark, the Spring-airs with laughing, swinging
and quaffing,
Bring, with flowering, blossoming, showering,
Freedom in binding, Life in finding!

Now the action sweeps on. Kings gather from neighbouring lands, bent on the capture of the country and the Queen. The most cunning of them uses as his figure head the handsome fellow who passes before the people as 'King', and by him the Queen is almost beguiled, but is left torn between doubt and despair. Then at the height of the festival the palace breaks into flames and in the conflagration the Queen sees the face of her Lord! That terrible sight strikes her heart with fear. She flies and seeks refuge with her father. But there the seven kings besiege him and defeat his forces. The kings claim her, but now at the hour of their triumph they are confounded and scattered. The King has come at last! We meet the proud and most cunning of the seven kings, alone at night on the road, with Grandfather (singing 'I am waiting with my all in the hope of losing everything…') and the Queen, humbled yet no longer despairing.

The last scene of all is in the Dark Chamber, where the bride-Queen seeks to serve at the feet of her Lord, yet knows His incomparable love lives within herself.

The King : 'I open the doors of this dark room today. The game is finished here! Come into the light!' The Queen : 'Before I go, let me bow at the feet of my Lord of darkness, my cruel, my terrible, my peerless one!'

THE DRAMA, THE MELODIES AND WORDS

If singers and listeners-readers have enjoyed the drama's narrative and songs, they may wish to know more of the drama, melodies and words of 'Raja', 'The King of the Dark Chamber'.

As a drama, 'Raja' moves the beholder by its action and by Tagore's recasting of the traditional Asian symbolism of King, bride-Queen and people, also found in the Bible from Solomon to Paul. It is a fine song-play, from its lively opening, through its development with gaiety and mystery, excitement and pathos, to its climax and close. It is accessible in English words although these are poor and are not by the author.[1] Before playing it in English, with its songs, a retranslation of the dialogue should be attempted. The play is not without faults but these could be cut. And though, speaking as a witness and 'walker-on', I enjoyed the playwright-producer's reappearance on the stage because his boys and girls so loved their joyful 'grandfather' singing with them, a producer would do well to read Edward Thompson's critical praise (see E. Thompson, 'Rabindranath Tagore : Poet and Dramatist', 2nd rev. ed. 1948).

As to the fine melodies and their modes, it will be seen that broadly the first, second and fourth are in the major doh or Ionian Mode, while the other two are in the minor (7-note) form of the re or Dorian Mode. (That is, if the doh mode be played as a scale on C, then using the 'white notes' of a piano for both, the re mode is a scale on D).[2] Yet treatment and mood differ in the three major melodies. The dramatic sequence is also enhanced by the change of rhythm through these songs.

As to the words of the songs, they may be taken in order, with an indication of their setting in the seasons, the changing landscape and the response of the people's customs, so significant in meaning. Every song has its allusions, instantly grasped by the Bard's fellow-countrymen. Where such instantaneous comprehension is vital as you listen, the English should bring in the latent image, suggest the customary act or name a quality present to Bengali eyes but absent to ours. What follows are commentaries on the translations, for singer and listener have a right to know how near or far these words may be to literal meanings or to imaged concepts, and to the sounds and rhythms of the music.

1. *Oh the gateways of the south are opening, let fling*

After the ripening and reaping of the paddy in the winter's clear sunshine and warmth, slowly, tree by tree, the browning leaves have been rustling to the dry ground. Then in mid-April come light breezes from the south, with swirling eddies, stirred (they say) by goblins. And suddenly on the jungle boughs, all bare but for those of dusty evergreens, the blossom bursts. The vermilion Gold Mohur and the Flame of the Forest, so readily mistaken for a forest fire! Spring's beauty is passionate. The days are already hot, and it is a joy to swing and feel the pulse of cooling air on cheek and limb. As Tagore said to me when producing his song-play of Spring, the Indian spring is poignant because so brief. And it is frightening for, as the petals that litter the hard earth wither, there comes the fiery heat of the hot weather, bringing thirst, hunger and fear that if the monsoon fails again there will be famine. Yet the New Year hopes, the free-time visiting, dancing, piping, quarrelling and lovemaking make spring a time of joy!

From the Poet's flow of metaphor one has been omitted : 'Come in thy new and beautiful chariot along the bakul strewn path'.

The white petals of the bakul (Mimusops Elengi) are unknown to us, like those of other flowers named. Nor do we know the form of an Indian chariot or car, still familiar to a Bengali villager from the terracotta friezes of little temples, and no doubt 'green' if bedecked with young foliage. Instead the first metaphor of the swing, a favourite in play and song and a ritual to bring rain with the south wind, is continued, or we should miss its full significance.

2. *Oh, we're rajas-royal, one and all*

The unison chorus was sung with delight by the children, for every child rejoices to feel he is a little king! Instead of substituting English words, 'kinglet' and 'king', I have kept to 'rajas' and 'raja', as all will understand who have

---

1. This translation is available as a free download at www.gutenberg.org/ebooks/6521.

2. Arthur Geddes planned to include a section on modes in this book, but did not live to complete it. Readers may wish to refer to the section on modes in his book *The Songs of Craig and Ben* Vol.2, p.74-79. William MacLellan, Glasgow 1961 (eds.)

lived in some minute feudatory raj. In this way the joy-ous image is unstrained and all are royal in the Kingdom. And as they sang the stanzas too, the children under-stood. For in spite of caste, the message sung is a part of India's highest traditions. Thoughtfully, in words I noted and kept, the Bard translated from the last stanza, 'And none of us shall meet our end, or doom, in the loathsome eddy of futility, or frustration'. In song the metaphor is simply told. It is that of crossing a Bengal river in flood, to reach the Meeting, the Union of all the Divine.

3. *Deep in my heart He dwells*

After the ringing authentic major of 'Oh we're rajas' an austere Dorian melody bears the faith born of inmost ex-perience : 'Deep in my heart He dwells'. Through search-ing and grief, the Maid's love is sustained by the realisation that He is 'ever and everywhere'. The first line of the melody, pausing long on the tonic re, moves qui-etly round it in the Plagal range. Then in a short bar, the sharpened third of 'seeking' impels the rise to the fourth, the subdominant, followed by the fall to the tragic minor third, on 'vain'. The melody descends on 'Deep in my eyes'. with an echo of the minor third, and closes on the opening phrase.

4. *Night fills my window*

This song, with its imagery of the unshuttered window open to the stars and a tiny light, is followed by 'Whither..?' In the melody of 'Night' there is a quiet movement around the tonic doh, steady rhythm and long-sustained final notes. In contrast is the re mode of 'Whither…?', with shifting lead to sol, the fourth, and the broken rhythm of restless quavers in 3:2, 3:2,…., for its unquiet search. The words of 'Night' are simple and, but for the first three words of introduction, allowed an al-most literal translation.

5. *Whither, wayward flying?*

This song, with its restless searching expressed in flitting imagery, subtle rhythms, needs freer translation to be-come song anew. In the printed English version of the play, the Poet sketched the concepts in slightly different images and prose and so quite naturally some of his words there came of themselves into my English song-verse. Here, with synonyms needed for close approach to its original significance, is a literal translation : 'Whither, out away, do they go on flying? Alas, alas! My restless eyes as forest birds to the wilderness flying away? Ah, heart, when charms (or fascinates) the play of the flute, then unguided, wandering, weeping, you would put on (no garland but) a noose, going hither and there, as to die. (Ah eyes, as forest birds --). Look, behold, (through the) door of the heart, who comes and goes? What news does the south wind bring that you listen for? Today the scent of blossom, laugh of happiness, song of eagerness! Though crazy-seeming the ever-lasting (ever-renewing) spring of the heart's wanderings and searching'.

The forms of the Bard's song-verse are hinted at by the English rhyming and near-rhyming. In the first line half-remembered sounds, re-echoing in my ear after nearly forty years, had blurred to perfect rhymes, although when reread they prove to be near-rhymes, vowel-rhymes, which are more subtle and freer, as in 'listening, singing'. 'Perfect rhymes' are also found in the original. Were any reader, with his eyes on the literal translation just given, to accuse me of infidelity to the original, its maker himself might simply smile and say, 'Of course, this verse transla-tion of my poem is imperfect. So was the English prose I wrote. And my Bengali song itself is but an echoing and rhymed re-echoing of sounds half-heard and images half-seen that finally, I know not how, took form in my song!'

II. SEVEN SONGS OF PRAYER, RESOLUTION AND MOURNING

Could a few words sum up the quest of a lifetime, they might be these. Rabindranath saw life as a unity, through intuition and meditation and in relationships shared with man and woman, in youth and age. And he found fulfilment by thought, work and art, and in the renewal of earth for the Divine latent in mankind. Of all these he sang.

For the seven songs which follow, something is told of their concepts and imagery, and the intimate associations of these with melodic tradition, linked to hour, season and mood in the life of the Bard and his people. While some singers or readers may turn straight to the songs and their verses, others may prefer to begin here. The singer or reciter will find that the listeners respond to a few words telling of the scene in which the song was conceived and created. Notes are given on the melodic mode of each song.

1. Ah my soul searches afar

The first seven notes hint, even to the uninitiated, at the song's mood of longing. And to an Indian ear they convey the morning hour of worship, to which the mode with its variants is consecrated. Rabindranath would say that this raga was associated with the ascetic, with meditative longing for self-less and attainment of all, atonement. The undertone of the Bengali words, translated in 'The Gardener' (no.5) as 'I am restless', suggests not the restlessness of childhood but of the ascetic who would leave the now for the ever, the near for the far, the far within. When I had played this lovely melody to monks of the Ramakrishna Brotherhood who were my hosts in their Himalayan retreat, a senior swami, a valued friend, said 'I will dance Bhairabi for you', and rising, he moved slowly with rhythmic motion of arms and hand, while we watched his silent expressive prayer. Now in strict classical tradition this mode is associated with Sivaite ritual by women and a variant of it with the solitary ascetic. But for Tagore the mode itself conveyed the essence of his mood and his fellow countryman, the swami, shared his feeling.

In this mode the final note, mi, never quite brings a sense of finality and there is no fundamental fifth, no true dominant. Hence 'threshold' notes leading to the fundamental five (or here four) are not heard in the opening and closing phrase or refrain around the note mi, except as mere passing notes. Not until the melody rises through to doh, through 'long' to 'endure', is ti, the fifth, accented. In the second part, starting very low, no threshold note is emphasised except at the close, on fa-mi. The third part rises from mi to accented doh, moving gently upward to around upper mi, from which it slowly descends, with hesitation around the minor third (sol, with sharpened threshold fa-sol), before the three descending notes into the final sol-fa mi, on 'sealed my door'.

The Bard sang this, as always, with very smooth time. The 'ornaments' are not sung as separate notes, but float, in smoothly passing microtones, around the note they emphasise. The words are close to the Bengali, except where the Poet's English seemed best. The only departure from literal meaning, the couplet 'Insistent as pain, Thy floating refrain', is suggested by the intensity of the Bard's own unforgettable singing.

2. Ah my master, I know not Thy own singing

This is a chanted utterance. Even the verse, though its rhyming pattern follows the original, is best read as free verse. It is the only one of the songs here which seems to echo the scale-form of a classical western aria, though not its regular structure. When sung with steady sustained expression, the melody can carry the utterance nobly. Dr Arnold Bake told me that it was the significance of the words which led him to place this song first in his anthology 'Chansons de Tagore' (Geuthner, Paris 1935). The sharp alliterations of the original are recalled by pointed syllables such as 'teach', 'tell'. The plea explicit in the second is implicit in the opening line. In Bengali Tagore had sung 'I wonder' and 'How dost thou sing, my Master?' In English he wrote 'I know not how Thou singest, my Master' (Gitanjali, no.3). Of the two forms, it was his English which came nearer to fitting the rhythm of the melody and led to the rhyming which he found, and I have sought in song.

Tagore's prose rendering loses one noble metaphor of his original. After 'breaking stones in speed', as in the Himalayan torrents in monsoon spates and flood, there 'flows onward the holy river of music'. Joyous attainment is associated with the great rivers and, rushing from the mountains, the Ganges flows in calm over the plains. And all over India confluence is symbolic of union with the Divine, suggesting the word 'joined'. In the English the vowel-rhyming avoids final consonants false to the flow of the original. As the metre and the timing of the melody is irregular, so is that of the original and the translation. Yet, when the third entry of the refrain is made one beat ahead of its expected place, it is because of the urgency of its appeal. Such songs are sung by wandering mendicant hermits or friars, the Baul singers of Hindu Bengal, men who have left or lost home for ever, in search of the unknown, God.

In the melody, which is a form of the major or doh mode, listen for the two threshold notes, the sharp seventh leading to the tonic (si-doh), for the sharpened fourth leading up to the fifth or dominant, and for the sighing descent fa-mi. This halting of one's expectation or hope for resolution on the tonic, or on the dominant sol, seems the clue to the yearning in the melody. Not once does it reach the upper tonic, except in passing quavers. In Part B, the ascent from the lower fifth or dominant is solemn : 'Deeply I long, or yearn, to join in Thy melody, or strain'.

3. Silent art Thou

The melody stands out for its entrancing compelling play of three and then of twice two quavers, with a carry-over (or syncopation) to the next three. It must be sung true to time. For 7/8 or 3/8 the Bard himself, while gently marking the main beats with hand and supple wrist, would keep the quavers true to time by marking them with the thumb on the inter-joints of the middle finger. Some such discipline seems needed if the time is not to degenerate to three main even beats, with the first as a mere triplet. The song's sustained urgency, rising to passionate appeal in 'Startle, quicken, shock me' owes much to this 7/8 measure. One would expect each opening phrase of 'three' to be repeated but instead the next and the following phrase step on after only two quavers each,

before the new bar opens. There is an element of disquiet in the search for a final note. One expects to close on the first note, the tonic, but one is led by a sharpened fourth to a concluding fifth.

The words keep close to the Bengali and render something of accents, smooth to begin with, marked with the growing intensity of 'Startle, shock, quicken'. As always the difficulty of English for singing is the lack of vowel-ending syllables. Thus bar 31 should literally begin 'Hearing (all) the stars sing their shining song... ' and the singer may sing this if he can, though 'a star' is nearer the vowel music of the Bard's song.

4. The bird, bulbul, sang to the flower, champa

This is a delicious little fantasy which the Bard would make me play for his pleasure and mine, but without my having yet attempted to translate in singing verse and so to understand. A bird, perhaps the gay flitting singer, the bulbul, asks the flower of the champa (frangipani), the last to bloom through the burning drought of May, why she is silent and can she hear his song? The flower replies 'He who can hear, He is not you, not you'. Then who? the listener may ask. I have allowed the translation to hint at the answer. If this is indeed in tune with the Bard's mood then, characteristically, he was quietly poking fun at himself, as a singer. 'Crazed by the aimless light hot breeze' and impatient of the infinite and silent mystery of the universe, of the world, of a flower! The time, with its pointed play of 5/8 quavers – 3/2 then 2/3 – is vital to this teasing mood. The two main alternating beats must be true to time although the Bard allowed himself delicate latitude with them, con rubato.

5. March alone! Stand alone!

This song was composed by Rabindranath in his prime, to rouse his fellow countrymen to stand up, to go forward, to face truth and utter it. None should fear alien power or outworn creeds, when either was false to mankind and truth. If need were, each must go forward, facing wounds, alone. The fire with which the Bard sang it was unforgettable. In the translation the direct word 'thou' is kept. First drafted direct from the Poet's singing, the English words are close to the original, except for the last fiery image. This may spring from a first searing recollection of the body of one newly dead, yet still dear and living to the son who has lit and must watch the consuming pyre. And it embodies a legend of the Mahabharata that a great sage gave his breast bone to form a thunderbolt, a 'thunder-fire', to save mankind. Although less easily grasped at a first hearing, the last lines may be sung : 'A bone of thy breast as the lightning, flashing, to light thy way alone!'

The fire, the snap and call of its marching vigour, the stern sol mode, that of the Scottish bagpipe, the resolve of 'Alone!' and the startling image at the climax, all these things may astonish some who only know the Poet's calm prose renderings in English. Its single-hearted courage made it sung in hours of hope or danger. Some six years after the Bard's death, his friend and spiritual comrade, the beloved Mahatma Gandhi, set out on foot in East Bengal and with a few unarmed men and women 'marched alone' through the seething villages facing fellow Indians maddened by incendiarism, lust and revenge. 'Alone' their stand, their march, their song; 'the truth, the truth', helped to halt bloodshed and restore calm.

The firm step is based on two beats to the bar (2/4) but as excitement mounts the Bard added a step, a beat (3/4), and at the climax the rhythm takes four full beats (4/4) returning to 2/4 at the end, The whole song was joyously sung in unison to 2/4 time throughout by the lads at Santiniketan in the spirit of 'March together', a fine but different thing. This unexpected, mounting change in beat conveys the sense of single-minded freedom. Although the 2/4 time has triplets, it must be 'snapped', with a true 'Scottish' or Bangla snap, as in the verse-lines (2/4) 'cry out clear…','jungle, jaggy', 'thunder'. The mode gives a full tone below the tonic except where, on leading to the refrain's repeat on 'none', this seventh rises towards the sharp by a microtone (or 'quarter tone') which comes instinctively in singing.

6. *Call me, ah call me never more*
In this song rings the anguish of utter loss when true love is given in vain. Union denied, no semblance of love is sought, for love is truth. In the original words one of the beauties of form lies in the rhymes which lead as in forewarning to the haunting refrain. In the rhythm the tie-over on 'Ah –' leads to the subtle change from triplets of 6/8 to the paired quavers on the first renunciation, 'never more, never', inviting the long note on 'more', echoed in its rocking repeat. From the simple minor mode of the first part, the second descends to a poignant characteristically Indian mode in which the inward-turning grief is expressed in ad-

jacent semitones. From this the song returns to the first mode, reaching a note higher, in final resolution.

7. *Though my time has come to leave now*
This was sung to me one sad monsoon day by my hostess, on her return from the funeral service for a dear friend at which it had been sung. It was for me an early sign of how closely the Bard's songs have been, for his fellow countrymen, their own, in joy and in sorrow. The mode with its changes of semitone on the second, above the first and final note, moves between the two minor modes, from la in rising, to mi in closing. And just before the refrain the poignancy is renewed with the subtle change in time of the accented second, on 'crying, "Come back".'

If these songs are sung by a people who, though reflective, are mainly illiterate, it is partly because each song is so self-contained, so simple. Taken singly, almost any of these poems or their melodies could be matched in the verse or airs of other poets or singers. Tagore not only rejoiced in the Sanskrit dramas of Kalidas and the heritage of modern Europe but in the lyrics of his own folk. Among the woods and wastes around Santiniketan he listened to the fluting of tribal herdboys, whose simple lyrics his friends and mine gathered and translated into their own Bengali because from Gurudev they had learned that the deepest things can be the simplest, What is rare is not only our Bard's matching of words and air, which helps to bring his voice to us in spite of the difficulties of our tongue and the imperfections of these translations. It is the range of his fellow feeling and perception, from sharing of human experience in friendship and intimacy to the discipline of solitary meditation. Solitude, instead of taking him away from other men and women, brought him back to them as brother, lover, parent, as listener and singer, as pupil, disciple, master.

Hence his search, his faith, was one throughout his life. The depth of his concern, alarm and grief grew within him as Europe and Americanised Japan crept, then plunged into total war, in a storm of hateful madness which was to sweep the shores of Bengal and of India like a disastrous tidal wave. Of this he spoke in his matchless Bengali on his eightieth birthday in 1941, a year of worldwide mourning. Of this he wrote in the last three months before his death. But of this he never sang. The face we loved was scarred. Its silence tells of a lover's grief for all mankind

AH MY SOUL SEARCHES AFAR – SEEKS THE DISTANCE . . .
Ami chan challo hé, ami sudur er piashi

AH MY MASTER, I KNOW NOT THY OWN SINGING!

Tumi kaemon ko-re gan koro je guni!

Very smoothly

trap my heart, close tie - ing, weav - ing round me deep sounds, still

ring - ing. Ah my Mas - ter, tell me, teach me of Thy sing - ing!

SILENT ART THOU, WHY?
Nirobe acho kaeno?

Andante. Very smoothly

Si - lent art Thou, why—— si——— lent? Ah, why——— si - lent?

Si - lent art Thou, why,——— why so? Out in the door - way, out in the door - way?

Si - lent art Thou, why——— why so? Dark - ened my eyes I——— can - not

see Thee be - fore me. Si - lent art Thou, why——— why so? Long - ing - ly shall I———

——— hear Thee, soon Thou wilt come, draw——— near me, thrust - ing my skiff a - float———

THE BIRD, BULBUL, SANG TO THE FLOWER, CHAMPA
Pakhi bo-le . . . . champa

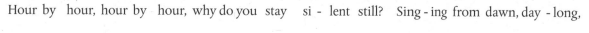

II

Dainty and white, fragrant and calm,
List'ning, the Champa gave reply.
"One who can hear, one who can hear,
His list'ning fills earth and sky!"

Bulbul sang on, "Spring, Spring!
Crazed by the breeze ,
Lightly I wing, wing, wing.
Still when I sing, sing, sing
Ah, if you hear, ah if you hear,
Why do you stay silent, why?"

MARCH ALONE! STAND ALONE!
Akla chelo re!

O–o even though all should leave thee,
Leave thee lone, to face the forest,
Lone, unlucky one, leave thee!
O break through the thickets of jungle, jaggy,
Break, with blood-reddened fe-et.
Tho' with blood-reddened fe-et! Still cleaving,
O tread out, O tread out, still tread out thy tra-ck!
Still tread thy way, alone!

Chorus

And when, in darkness and tempest,
Doors are barred and lamps are hidden,
Lamps are darkened and hidden,
Lightning flash, wi' thunder crashing,
Strike and burn thy body,
Thy spirit shall flay me within,
Till spirit and body, a brazier, burning,
Shall light thy way, alone!

Chorus

CALL ME, AH CALL ME NEVERMORE!

Deko na!

Andante

Call me, ah, —— call me ne-ver more, ne-ver more! Ah, ne-ver more! ——————

Now I go o-ver the ri-ver, o far a-way shore! Ne-ver-more! —— Gifts I gave of

love I bore, gave you how long a-go? ————————— Prof-fer me no re-

turn, ——————— no-thing for those you owe. —— Of-fer no alms to me,

mer-cy's no balm for my sor-row sore, ne-ver-more! ——— Wa-ter of grief, of

sor-row wash off my shame of los-ing. Know-ing you can-not

care, ——— do not veil truth, pre-ten-ding. Wa-ters of grief, of

sor-row, wash off my shame of los-ing. Know-ing you can-not

care, ——————— do not veil truth pre-ten-ding. Ah let no mem-or-y

ling - er   when I   am   gone and   far   a - way.   Do   not   ling   - er———

Ne - ver   call   me   to   meet you,   meet   you,   ne - ver   - more!———

THOUGH MY TIME HAS COME TO LEAVE NOW, STILL THEY CALL ME

. . . Pi-chu da-ke

Though my time has come to leave now,
Still they call me.

Flowing full t' the brim,
Dark waters surge to an unknown sea.
Swiflty flowing, they call me
Warning, soon is my time to leave now,
Yet recalling,
Though my time has come to leave now,
Still they call me.

III. Two Songs of Youth and Santiniketan

ROAD THAT LURES AWAY
Gram chara

At a walking pace - smoothly

Road, red road, tru-ant road that lures a - way, —— ah, lures ———— through the

ham - let, yon - der, a - way. —— Why do I hold out hands? To whom, —— where?

Tru - ant, my mind is lost in sands on the road that lures a - way. ——

From my home the red road draws me, va - ga - bond! Step by step, by

step, it draws me on, —— on, still on, be - yond. —— Ah, draw - ing me on, — it

leads me, turn by turn, —— draws me whi-ther, whi - ther, far, on the road that lures me a -

way. ———— May won -ders wait for me to see, to learn, —— dan - ger lurk, or

new ad - ven - ture stern?——— Where will it go, ere I the end dis -

cern?——— Tru - ant road, with turn on turn, you lure me on and a - way.———

The 'red road' of laterite leads away from Santiniketan and its cares!

OURS IS SHE – SANTI-NIKETAN
Amader Santiniketan!

Once, upon a journey, the 'Great Mystic' or 'Great Teacher', Maharshi Tagore, father of Rabindranath, halted to rest on the bare red-soiled upland a full hundred feet above the level green plain of Western Bengal, which stretches far to the blue horizon. There he found serenity, calm and peace. And it is told that as he sat alone, a lurking band of jungle brigands, dacoits, who had spied the traveller, were about to fall on the defenceless old man when, seeing him rapt in meditation and beholding the light that shone from his quiet unseeing eyes, they bowed instead and taking the dust off his feet, asked his blessing and crept away! Not long after, the Maharshi Tagore, purchasing the site from friends nearby, gave it a new name, from *santi*, peace, home of peace – Santiniketan. There the robust sal trees, when protected, grow as tall as in the wild woodland further away from the plain, and were gathered 'in company' with groves of low feathery-leaved amlaki, the phyllanthus.

The boy Rabindranath came to stay here and in his turn grew fond of its open horizons. Later, seeking a healthy spot, relatively free from malaria and deadly cholera, in which to bring up his own children, he founded a school for them and their friends in which both they and he would take active parts, and which would be nearer to his heart's desire for them and for the needs of their growing minds. And when in 1912, Rabindranath was awarded the Nobel Prize, he used the prize money to found the University of Santiniketan. This was to be at once truer to the spirit, the people and the soil of Bengal and India, than British founded institutions, and also to encourage wide, free intercourse with Europe and Asia. A mile down a 'red road', at the edge of the green plain, he founded a farm for rural reconstruction, Sriniketan.

It was for the boys and girls, the youths and maidens who lived here that the Bard composed this joyous song, 'Ours, our own, ours for all, is our Santiniketan'. There is no lovelier memory than of hearing it sung by them as night closed some joyous festival in which they had joined with their beloved Teacher, their Gurudev, They were attuned – like the harmonic love-strings of a sitar. In unison their young voices sang up joyously and unbidden, 'Ours is she, Santi-ni-ke-ta-n!...Brother to brother, a single soul! Santi-niketan!'

I know that at the dim end of some day the sun will bid me its last farewell.

Shepherds will play their pipes beneath the banyan trees, and cattle graze
    on the slope by the river, while my days will pass into the dark.

This is my prayer, that I may know before I leave why the earth called me to
    her arms.

Why her night's silence spoke to me of stars, and her daylight kissed my
    thoughts into flower.

Before I go may I linger over my last refrain, completing its music, may the
    lamp be lit to see your face and the wreath woven to crown you.

– from *Fruit-Gathering*